ALL ABOUT BUGS

Rotting wood
can be a great bug
habitat. This log has attracted
beetles, woodlice, millipedes, centipedes
and wasps. See if you can spot them!

ALL ABOUT BUGS

David Chandler

NEW HOLLAND

First published in 2008 by New Holland Publishers (UK) Ltd
London • Cape Town • Sydney • Auckland

www.newhollandpublishers.com

Garfield House, 86-88 Edgware Road, London W2 2EA, United Kingdom
80 McKenzie Street, Cape Town 8001, South Africa
Unit 1, 66 Gibbes Street, Chatswood, New South Wales, Australia 2067
218 Lake Road, Northcote, Auckland, New Zealand

ISBN 978 1 84773 051 0

Senior Editor: Krystyna Mayer
Design: Fetherstonhaugh (www.fetherstonhaugh.com)
Production: Melanie Dowland
Editorial Consultant: James Parry
Editorial Direction: Rosemary Wilkinson

NEW
HOLLAND

CONTENTS

WHAT IS A BUG?

This book is all about bugs. An entomologist (someone who studies insects) would say that a *true* bug was a particular type of insect, one that belonged to the order Hemiptera. But this book isn't just about these creatures – it's about small animals with six or more legs – including insects, spiders, mites, scorpions, woodlice, centipedes and millipedes.

These animals are small because they wear their skeletons on the outside rather than the inside! Their bodies are encased in an 'exoskeleton' made mostly of chitin (a type of carbohydrate). To grow, animals with an exoskeleton have to push their way out of their old 'skin', and wait while the new one hardens. If they were too big, they would collapse while they were waiting!

So far, scientists have described around a million species of 'bug'. This is more than all the different birds, mammals, fish, reptiles and amphibians put together. It might sound like a lot, but the fact is that there are probably millions more bug species still waiting to be discovered and given names.

Bugs come in many shapes and sizes and live in lots of different places. There are bugs in the air, on the ground and under the ground, on plants and inside plants, under water and walking on the water. There are gentle plant-eaters and fierce predators, small ones, bigger ones, bugs that are wonderfully camouflaged and bugs that are very brightly coloured. Some are poisonous or can sting, others just pretend that they can. Some live in colonies of millions, others

can produce
young without
mating.

Don't be fooled by the small sizes of bugs –
they are incredibly important and there are
lots of them. Someone worked out that
for each person on the planet, there
are around 200 million insects. That's
not counting all the other bugs, such as
spiders, woodlice and centipedes, which are
not insects!

Without bugs, the world would be a
very different place. Some bugs do
cause problems because they
carry diseases or damage stored foods or
timber. But bugs do lots of good things too. They are food for
many other animals, including some people. There are even plants
that eat them. Some are natural 'bin-men', clearing away dead animals
and plants and dung – imagine a world without them!

Many plants depend on bugs for pollination –
the bugs help turn flowers into fruits. Bugs
are also great to watch – all of them are
amazing creatures.

Bugs are fascinating, and wherever you
live, there are bugs nearby, just waiting
to be discovered!

BUG LIFECYCLES

The lifecycle of a butterfly or moth is quite well known. An adult lays eggs that hatch into caterpillars. A caterpillar turns into a pupa. Inside the pupa a miracle takes place – everything gets rearranged and out comes the adult insect. But there are plenty of bugs that do things differently.

The **Silverfish** (see page 14) lays eggs that hatch into miniature versions of the adult insect. Ten moults later, the Silverfish is fully grown.

The eggs of **Common Green Shield Bugs** (see page 23) hatch into larvae that look like small versions of the adult, but without the wings. The wings appear and grow as the larvae moult and get bigger.

Dragonfly and **damselfly** (see pages 16–17) eggs hatch into larvae or nymphs that live in water. They moult up to 15 times before becoming beautiful flying adults.

Adult and young shield bugs look similar.

Damselfly nymph

Adult damselfly

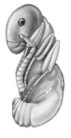

This bush cricket has wings (not all bush crickets do).
The wings get bigger as the insect gets older.

A female **spider** (see pages 56–8) wraps up her eggs in a silk case. Some spiders leave the case in a safe place and stay with it. Others take it with them wherever they go. When the eggs hatch tiny spiders come out. After five to ten moults they are fully grown.

Female **woodlice** (see page 59) are a bit like kangaroos – the eggs are stored and hatch in a pouch on the female's underside. A few days later the young emerge looking like small adults.

Millipedes (see page 62) lay their eggs in a nest. At first the young don't have a full set of legs – they only have three pairs. After a quick moult there are four more pairs. There are six more moults before they are fully adult, and more segments and legs are added every time they moult.

An ant's lifecycle: eggs, larva, pupa and adult.

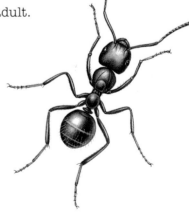

GOING BUG-EYED

There are lots of places where you can look for bugs and you don't need any special equipment to get started. Here are some things you could try:

- Think small and just start looking – you might be surprised at where you find bugs – there could be a **Zebra Spider** on a sunny wall or an **earwig** in the birdfeeder, for example!

- Try looking under logs and rocks for **centipedes**, **millipedes**, **woodlice** and **beetles**. Compost heaps can also be worth exploring.

- Look carefully around brightly coloured flowers – they often attract insects, including **bees** and **butterflies**. They also attract **moths**, and some moth species fly during the day.

- Check out the plants around ponds, lakes and rivers, and look at the water's surface. In summer you might see **dragonflies**, **damselflies**, **pond skaters** and **whirligig beetles**.

- You could try putting an old white sheet under a branch of a tree or bush. Give the branch a quick shake and see what sorts of bug fall onto the sheet.

- Search through areas of long grass. You could find **grasshoppers**, grass-loving **butterflies** and **moths**, and more.

- Many moth species are attracted to lights. If you're allowed, leave an outside light on overnight or leave the bathroom light on with the window open. Check it out in the morning – as well as **moths**, there could be **lacewings** and **ichneumon flies** resting near the light. Warm overcast summer evenings are particularly good times to do this.

- Try to watch bugs in their natural habitats rather than catching them – some are very fragile and could easily be harmed. Any creatures that you have caught should be well looked after and returned to where you found them as soon as possible. Take care not to damage the places where they live when you are looking for them, and leave logs and rocks in the positions you find them.

- A few plastic pots may be useful for holding bugs while you're looking at them, but don't keep bugs as pets. If you have to handle them, do so with great care. Picking them up with a small paintbrush will stop you squashing them with your fingers. You might want a magnifying glass too, but it's not essential.

- Whenever you are bug hunting, make sure that an adult knows where you are going and what you are doing. Why not try to get them interested too?

NAME THAT BUG!

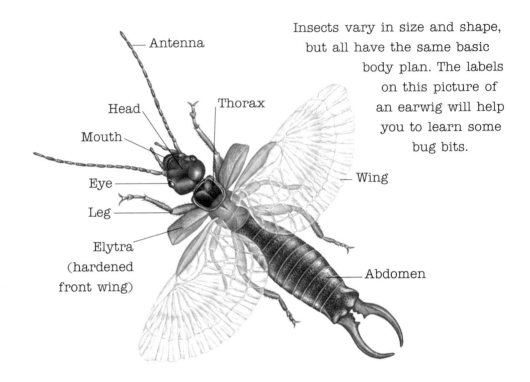

Insects vary in size and shape, but all have the same basic body plan. The labels on this picture of an earwig will help you to learn some bug bits.

Antenna

Head

Mouth

Thorax

Eye

Leg

Wing

Elytra
(hardened
front wing)

Abdomen

This book isn't big enough to cover all of the bugs that you might see – in the UK alone there are around 20,000 species of insect, and that doesn't include the spiders, woodlice, centipedes and millipedes.

The species in this book are mostly easy to see. They will give you a good idea of the variety that exists in the bug world. Although many of the bugs you will find won't be in here, this book should help you work out what group they are in. It will help you to know the difference between, for example, an insect and a spider, a centipede and a millipede, a spider and a harvestman, and a grasshopper and a bush cricket.

If you find a mystery bug, this table should help you to work out what it is. Remember that bug larvae can be very different from the adults. This table is about adult bugs only. It doesn't cover every bug group, but does cover the animals you are likely to find.

Happy bug-hunting!

Number of legs	Type of bug	Look for	Check out these pages
6	Insects (plus bristletails and springtails)	A large and very varied group. Most insects have two pairs of wings, but some only have one pair, and some don't have any. The insect body is divided into three parts as shown in the picture opposite. They are the head, thorax and abdomen.	14–54
8	Spiders	Body has two parts and an obvious waist.	56–8
8	Harvestmen	No waist. A lump on top of the body.	56
8	Mites and ticks	No waist. No lump on top of the body.	54
14	Woodlice	Overlapping 'armoured plates' along the top of the animal.	59–60
More than 14	Centipedes	One pair of legs on each body segment.	61
More than 14	Millipedes	Two pairs of legs on most body segments.	62

SILVERFISH
LEPISMA SACCHARINA

Did you know?
Silverfish eat flour, paper, photographs and the glue in book bindings and food cartons. They can live for a year without eating!

When to see Any time of year. Mostly active at night. Check out your kitchen or bathroom at night.

Where to see Common in Britain. Likes damp places in houses.

What to look for Flattened, tapering body about 20 mm long. Wingless body is covered in silvery scales, which make it slippery and help it to escape from spiders and ants. Look for Silverfish wriggling at speed across the floor.

TWO-TAILED BRISTLETAIL
CAMPODEA FRAGILIS

When to see Any time of year.

Where to see Common across Britain and found on every continent apart from Antarctica. Look for it in compost heaps and among rotting plant material.

What to look for A small creature up to about 6 mm long with a long body, six legs, long antennae and two 'tails'. It has no wings and no eyes, but it doesn't like the light. May be found in groups.

Did you know?
Scientists no longer think this is an insect. It's in another group of animals called Hexapods. They have six legs but their mouthparts are different from those of true insects. Some of them also have simple, leg-like structures on the abdomen as well as the legs on the thorax.

POND OLIVE – A MAYFLY

CLOEON DIPTERUM

When to see Adults fly from May to October. Most are active at dawn and dusk or at night.

Where to see Common in Britain and on the Continent. Look around small areas of still water, including ponds and water butts.

What to look for Delicate insect about 13 mm long, including two tails (many mayfly species have three tails). It has one pair of wings (most mayflies have two pairs, with the front ones being the biggest), tiny antennae and very long front legs. The front edges of the female's wings are brownish. The male has big eyes that are higher than the rest of its head. This is one of 51 mayfly species found in Britain.

Did you know?

Adult mayflies don't feed. They live for a few days at most (less than an hour in some species). Mayfly nymphs live in water.

Side view of species with two pairs of wings.

COMMON BLUE DAMSELFLY
ENALLAGMA CYATHIGERUM

When to see End of April to October.

Where to see Common in most of Britain and on the Continent around slow-flowing rivers, lakes and ponds.

What to look for Damselflies are delicate insects with long thin abdomens and separated eyes. All four wings are similar in size and shape. At rest their wings are held folded along the abdomen, or partly open. The Common Blue Damselfly has a blue and black abdomen with a black 'mushroom' shape near the thorax and broad blue stripes on the thorax. 29–36 mm long.

Did you know?

The Common Blue Damselfly is probably found in more parts of Europe than any other damselfly or dragonfly.

LARGE RED DAMSELFLY
PYRRHOSOMA NYMPHULA
This bright red damselfly is found in most of Europe, in many habitats. Areas of still water with lots of plants are particularly good places to look for it. In Britain it is normally the first damselfly to emerge in spring. About 35 mm long.

SOUTHERN HAWKER
AESHNA CYANEA

When to see June to October, and especially July and August.

Where to see Common in much of Europe. Rare in Scotland, and only one record from Ireland. Breeding sites include garden ponds and other small and shady pools. It hunts in sunny patches in woods, by hedgerows and in gardens.

What to look for The 'true' dragonflies are much stouter than damselflies (see opposite). Their hind wings are bigger than their forewings, and they rest with their wings open. Most species' eyes are not separated. The Southern Hawker is large, with a wingspan of around 100 mm. A mature male has big 'headlights' on the thorax, blue and green spots on the abdomen and blue stripes at the tail end of the abdomen. 67–76 mm long.

Did you know?
Southern Hawkers can be a bit nosy – sometimes they will fly very close to people for a better look!

COMMON FIELD GRASSHOPPER
CHORTHIPPUS BRUNNEUS

Did you know?
If grasshoppers are caught by a predator they will kick with their strong hind legs and throw up!

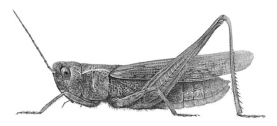

Many grasshopper species lay their eggs underground using their stretchy, bendy abdomen. The soil needs to be soft, though!

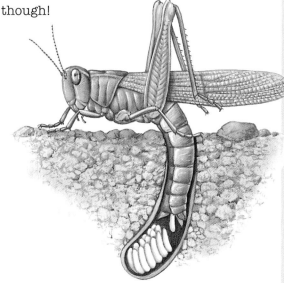

When to see Sunny days between June and October.

Where to see Common in Britain, northern Europe and central Europe. Found in dry grassland, often with bare patches of earth.

What to look for Can be black, purple or different shades of green or brown. The narrow wings are longer than the abdomen, and the underneath of the thorax is hairy. Listen for its song: a short chirp repeated 6–10 times, with roughly 2-second intervals. About 20 mm long. It is one of Britain's 30 grasshopper and cricket species.

BLUE-WINGED GRASSHOPPER

OEDIPODA CAERULESCENS

When to see July to November.

Where to see Dry warm areas in central and southern Europe. Sand dunes are a good place to look for them. In Britain found only on Jersey and Guernsey.

What to look for A flash of blue and black on a grasshopper that flies away from you and then disappears. The colours are on the hind wings. About 17–26 mm long.

Did you know?

The coloured wings are used to confuse predators, who still look for the bright colour even when the grasshopper lands suddenly, closes its wings and 'changes' colour.

SPECKLED BUSH CRICKET
LEPTOPHYES PUNCTATISSIMA

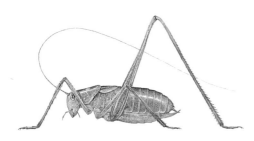

Did you know?

Unlike most bush crickets, the males and females sing. The song is short, weak, scratchy and hard for humans to hear.

Alien-like head has very long antennae, which help it to find food in the dark.

When to see July to November. Look for them coming to bright lights or windows after dark. Look on garden plants, too – although they are very well camouflaged.

Where to see Common in southern and eastern England. Also found in central and southern Europe.

What to look for Very long back legs and very long, thin antennae. This cricket is green with lots of red speckles. Both sexes have a brown stripe on the back, although the female's is very thin. Their forewings are very short – they can't fly. The female has an obvious curved ovipositor at the rear end. The male is 10–15 mm long, the female 20–25 mm long. One of 10 bush cricket species found in Britain.

Cricket lifecycle: from egg to adult. This species is winged and can fly, unlike the Speckled Bush Cricket.

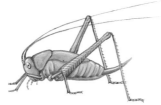
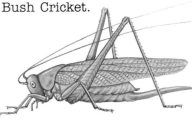

Did you know?

Female Praying Mantises sometimes eat the males (head first) before, during or after mating. Mantises catch moving insects, so if an insect stays still it is safe.

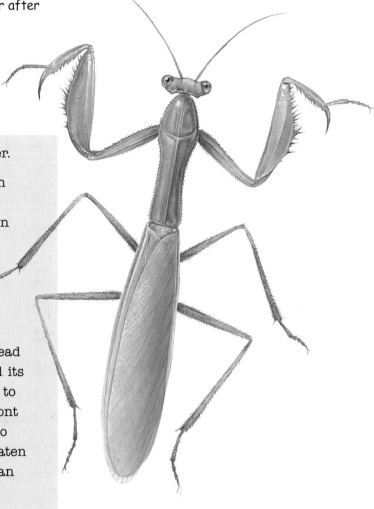

When to see July to November.

Where to see Scrub and rough grassy areas in central and southern Europe. Not found in Britain.

What to look for Large green or brown insect with long wings and long legs. It lies in wait and ambushes its prey. Its head is very mobile and large, and its well-separated eyes enable it to track passing insects. The front legs are spiky and dart out to spear insect prey, which is eaten alive. The male is thinner than the female. 40–70 mm long.

COMMON EARWIG
FORFICULA AURICULARIA

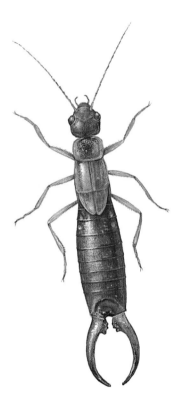

When to see Any time of year. Active at night, hiding under rocks, logs and in other nooks and crannies during the day.

Where to see Common in Britain and on the Continent. Found in many different habitats.

What to look for A long brown insect with an abdomen that is darker than the rest of its body. Males and females have pincers at the end of the abdomen – the male's pincers are more curved than the female's. The female is very maternal. She lays 20–50 eggs in soil and cares for them during winter. After the young hatch, she feeds and cares for them until they are fully developed and can leave their nest. 10–14 mm long.

Did you know?
Male earwigs use their pincers to fight other males and to warn off hedgehogs and shrews that might eat them. They will use them on people as well, but it shouldn't hurt too much!

COMMON GREEN SHIELD BUG
PALOMENA PRASINA

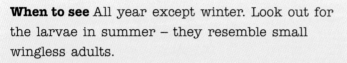

When to see All year except winter. Look out for the larvae in summer – they resemble small wingless adults.

Where to see Common in woods, hedgerows, grasslands and gardens in much of Europe, although they are harder to see in Scotland than in England.

What to look for The adult is a shield-shaped green bug 10–15mm long, with brown wingtips visible over the rear of its abdomen.

Did you know?

In autumn this bug turns more brown in colour and then hibernates. It comes out again in spring – but turns green again first! Great camouflage all year round!

Shield-bug larvae look like miniature versions of adults.

COMMON GREEN CAPSID

LYGOCORIS PABULINUS

When to see May to October.

Where to see Common throughout Britain on many different plants. Soft fruit plants such as raspberry are a good place to look for them.

What to look for Smaller and different in shape from the Common Green Shield Bug. It is green, with brown wing tips visible over the tail end of the abdomen (on adults). The larvae are more or less completely green. Less than 10 mm long.

Raspberries are a favourite food plant.

Did you know?

The males court the females by vibrating their abdomens. This seems to be triggered by 'pheromones' – chemical substances attracting the males – on the females' legs.

COMMON POND SKATER
GERRIS LACUSTRIS

When to see April to October. Adults hibernate in winter.

Where to see Ponds, lakes and slow-moving rivers across Europe.

What to look for A small brown-black insect skating over the water's surface. It uses its middle legs to move forwards, back legs to steer and front legs to grab insect food, which can be dead or alive. It senses vibrations made by another insect and quickly 'paddles' to its next meal. 8–10 mm long.

Did you know?
Pond skaters have water-repellent hairs. These help them to walk on water and keep them dry when they dive.

WATER SCORPION
NEPA CINEREA

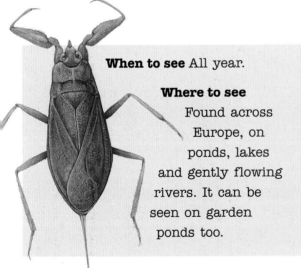

When to see All year.

Where to see Found across Europe, on ponds, lakes and gently flowing rivers. It can be seen on garden ponds too.

What to look for A flat, impressive insect with scorpion-like front legs and a snorkel at the back end. It's not a good swimmer. Instead, it walks slowly over plants or mud just under the water, using its snorkel to breathe. Surprisingly, under the wing cases there's a pink abdomen and wings. About 20 mm long.

Did you know?
Water Scorpions can fly but most of them never do – but if they are forced to fly to find a new home then they will.

GREAT WATER BOATMAN or
COMMON BACKSWIMMER *NOTONECTA GLAUCA*

Did you know?

It's light that tells them which way up to swim. In an aquarium with lights at the bottom only, they swim the right way up.

When to see Any time of year.

Where to see Common in ponds, lakes and slow-flowing rivers across Britain and continental Europe.

What to look for A bug that swims on its back! It is 14–17 mm long with a dark spot on its brown back, and swims with an air bubble on its 'belly'. A fierce predator, it eats tadpoles and very small fish. Take care if you catch one pond dipping – they can give you a nasty nip! It can fly and may appear in newly created garden ponds. Lesser Water Boatmen are similar, but swim the right way up and are plant-eaters.

Swims upside down, 'rowing' with its back legs.

COMMON FROGHOPPER
PHILAENUS SPUMARIUS

When to see June to October.

Where to see Found on many different plants throughout Britain and continental Europe.

What to look for Most adults are brown with darker markings, but some are green, yellowish or even black. Look for 'cuckoo-spit' (a white frothy substance) on plants. Froghopper larvae make this for protection from predators and from drying out. The bubble liquid is actually the sap of the plant that has passed right through the larva. 5–6 mm long.

The name 'froghopper' derives from its appearance – the adults look a bit like frogs from above and also jump very well!

Did you know?
Cuckoo spit may sound like a safe place for a froghopper larva – but there are solitary wasps that have worked out that there could be food inside.

GREEN LACEWING
CHRYSOPA PALLENS

Did you know?

It's a gardeners' friend: Green Lacewings
eat aphids, which can be a garden pest.

When to see May to August, flying mostly at night.

Where to see Anywhere with lots of plants, including gardens and woods.
Common in most of Europe, but not found in Scotland. Attracted to lights at
night and will come into houses.

What to look for Delicate green insect with big lacy wings, long antennae and
golden eyes. When resting, the wings are held like a tent over the body.
Green Lacewings are easy to identify, but there are two other very similar
lacewing species in the UK. About 20 mm long.

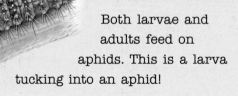

Both larvae and
adults feed on
aphids. This is a larva
tucking into an aphid!

Did you know?

Caddis fly cases may be
made of snail shells.
Sometimes the snails are
still alive!

When to see Mostly spring to
autumn, especially at dusk. This
species flies from May to November.

Where to see Almost anywhere with still or moving fresh water. The adults
are also attracted to lights. This species uses small ponds for breeding and is
common throughout Britain. It is one of 198 British species.

What to look for Caddis flies have hairy bodies and wings, long antennae and
long legs with spurs on. At rest they hold their wings over their bodies like
tents. Look for swarms of recently emerged adults dancing in columns.
Caddis fly larvae live underwater. Most make tubes from bits of plants,
stones, sand or snail shells to live in. The cases provide good camouflage and
protect the larvae from predators. This species is about 35 mm long,
excluding its antennae.

At rest caddis flies look
a bit like moths.

COMMON or SEPTEMBER CRANE FLY

TIPULA PALUDOSA

Did you know?

The adults are completely harmless, but the larvae (called leatherjackets) live in the soil and can damage crops.

When to see Any time of year, although it is most common in autumn. The adults are most active at night.

Where to see Common on grasslands and in gardens across Britain. They will come inside houses.

What to look for This is *the* Daddy-long-legs, although other crane flies look similar. It has long legs (which come off easily, so take care if you have to handle one), and one pair of wings. Its second pair of wings is reduced to 'halteres', which help it to balance in flight. Its wings are brownish with a brown line along the front edge. The female's abdomen ends in a point. This is the ovipositor, used for laying eggs in the soil. About 25 mm long.

Female of some crane-fly species lays eggs by bouncing on the soil. This allows her to pick up enough speed to prick the soil with her ovipositor and leave the eggs behind.

ST MARK'S FLY
BIBIO MARCI

When to see Sunny days between late April and June.

Where to see Gardens, grasslands, hedgerows, woodlands and roadside verges. Common throughout Britain.

What to look for A swarm of black flies, all with obvious long dangling legs. The legs make the flies look heavy in flight. They can also be seen sunning themselves on walls and flowers. They are about 11 mm long, with a black body, reddish eyes and a glossy thorax. The male has very big eyes, making its head look bigger than the female's. The larvae live in the soil, where they eat rotting material and the roots of plants. They are frequently found in compost heaps. The adults feed on nectar.

Did you know?
It's called the St Mark's Fly because the adults often make their first appearance of the year around 25 April, which is St Mark's Day.

BEE FLY
BOMBYLIUS MAJOR

When to see April to October.

Where to see Common in gardens, hedgerows and woods over much of Britain, although harder to see further north. Look for hovering Bee Flies around spring flowers.

What to look for A fly that looks like a bee – it mimics small bumblebees. Brown furry body, long legs and a long, mean-looking proboscis that is used for sucking nectar. The wings are dark along the front edges. Listen for a high-pitched humming noise when it hovers. 10–12 mm long.

Did you know?
Bee Flies lay their eggs near the nests of wasps and solitary bees. The larvae move into the nests, and eat the food that's been stored there and the larvae of the bees and wasps.

CELERY FLY
EULEIA HERACLEI

Did you know?
The Celery Fly's eyes change colour when it's dead. Its lovely green eyes turn reddish.

When to see April to November.

Where to see Common across Britain, including in gardens. Look for it around Umbellifers (plants of the carrot family). Check parsnip and celery plants, where this species can be a pest because the larvae damage the leaves.

What to look for A small picture-wing fly about 6 mm long. Its wing pattern and body colour can be very dark brown or a lighter brown. The female has a pointed 'tail' and a stiff ovipositor for egg laying. The eyes are green.

Syrphus ribesii

Scaeva pyrastri

When to see This species can be seen on sunny days between April and November.

Where to see Common in gardens, hedgerows and woods throughout Britain and continental Europe.

What to look for Many hoverflies look like wasps or bees. They hover and dart around in the air. This one is a wasp-like insect that may occur in large numbers. Look for it drinking nectar from a flower or hovering near blossoms. It is about 10 mm long. There are about 270 hoverfly species in Britain. Two others are shown here. They don't have common names – only the long scientific ones!

Volucella zonaria

Did you know?

Many hoverfly species' larvae eat aphids, so they're a gardener's friend.

BLUEBOTTLE

CALLIPHORA VOMITORIA

Did you know?

To feed, Bluebottles dribble on their food. Their saliva breaks down the food and then they slurp it up.

When to see All year round.

Where to see Common across Britain and on the Continent. Can be seen around houses, gardens, woods and hedgerows. Look for Bluebottles sunning themselves on walls. The females will lay eggs in fish, meat and animal wounds. The males can often be seen on flowers, feeding on the nectar.

What to look for Hairy insect with shiny blue bands on abdomen, black legs and black patches under brownish eyes. It is generally the females that come into houses, looking for meat or fish left out of the fridge in which to lay their eggs. The larvae then feed on the food. The males are happier outdoors sipping nectar. Bluebottle larvae are creamy white and carrot shaped. Since these flies feed on dead or dying material they are a useful part of the lifecycle of a garden. They clear up the rubbish left behind by others, including humans! The adults are about 10 mm long.

HORNTAIL or WOOD WASP

UROCERUS GIGAS

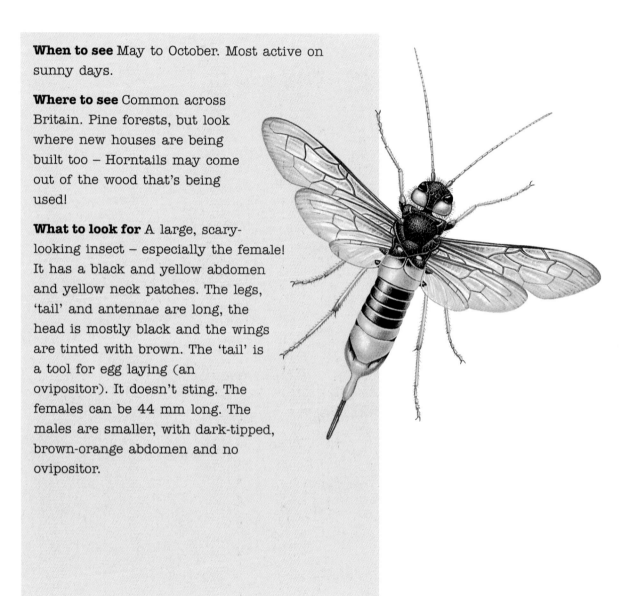

When to see May to October. Most active on sunny days.

Where to see Common across Britain. Pine forests, but look where new houses are being built too – Horntails may come out of the wood that's being used!

What to look for A large, scary-looking insect – especially the female! It has a black and yellow abdomen and yellow neck patches. The legs, 'tail' and antennae are long, the head is mostly black and the wings are tinted with brown. The 'tail' is a tool for egg laying (an ovipositor). It doesn't sting. The females can be 44 mm long. The males are smaller, with dark-tipped, brown-orange abdomen and no ovipositor.

Did you know?

A female uses her ovipositor to drill up to 10 mm into wood to lay her eggs. It is two or three years before the adults come out of the wood.

BEDEGUAR GALL WASP
DIPLOLEPIS ROSAE

When to see Adults are active from April to June but are hard to see. Look for the galls from summer to early autumn.

Where to see Common in Britain and northern continental Europe. Gall wasps lay their eggs on the Dog Rose. When the eggs hatch, the rose forms a gall around the larvae. The gall protects the larvae and provides food for them. Look for the gall (a Bedeguar Gall or Robin's Pincushion) on Dog Roses in gardens and the countryside.

What to look for The galls look like small balls of greenish or reddish hairs. The adults are about 4 mm long, and black with an orange abdomen and legs.

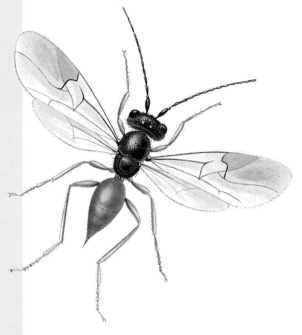

Did you know?

These insects don't need to mate to lay eggs! The males are hard to find – for each male, there are hundreds of females.

The gall is a protective covering for the larvae.

ICHNEUMON FLY
NETELIA TESTACEA

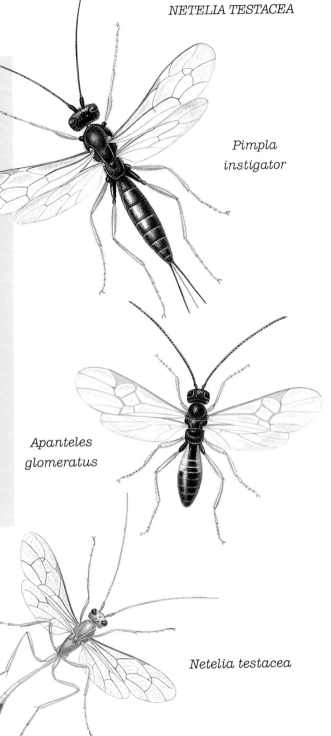

When to see Summer nights. They are attracted into houses by lights.

Where to see Common in well-vegetated areas across Britain and on the Continent.

What to look for Orange insect with long legs and antennae. The abdomen has a dark tip and curves upwards. The ovipositor (for egg laying) is short, but it can get through human skin, so if you ever need to handle the insect, do so with care! The wings have orange triangles on the front edge. About 20 mm long. This is one of about 4,000 species of ichneumon fly in Europe! Two other species are shown here.

Pimpla instigator

Apanteles glomeratus

Did you know?

This ichneumon fly lays its eggs on the outsides of moth caterpillars. The eggs hatch, and the larvae gradually eat the caterpillar.

Netelia testacea

SMALL BLACK ANT

LASIUS NIGER

Ant
lifecycle

Eggs

Larva

Pupa

Adult

Ants may be seen
carrying food along
a trail to their nest.

Did you know?

Flying ants are males and queens that are intent on mating. After the queen has mated she breaks off her wings. She may wait until the following spring before starting a new colony.

When to see The Small Black Ant lives in colonies of thousands that survive from year to year. It is especially obvious when winged forms appear (flying ants) on warm days in July or August. Workers, which are wingless, are often seen at other times too.

Where to see Common across Britain and continental Europe in many habitats including gardens. May nest under paths and in walls, and comes into houses looking for sweet foods.

What to look for This is the dark-coloured (dark brown or black) garden ant. It has a big head and abdomen. The waist is narrow with only one segment. Workers are about 5 mm long.

RED ANT

MYRMICA RUBRA

This is another common ant species seen in gardens. The workers are red-brown. Unlike Small Black Ants, Red Ants can sting.

When to see Late spring to autumn.

Where to see Common across Britain and continental Europe in many habitats, including gardens.

What to look for Most of the wasps you see are workers. These are about 10 mm long. Look for yellow stripes and four yellow spots on the thorax. The abdomen is black and yellow, and there is a black 'anchor' on the front of the face. Queens and males are larger than workers. The males only appear late in the season. May sting if provoked.

Workers collect wood pulp, the raw material for their nest.

Did you know?

The workers and males die in autumn. Only the queens make it through the winter, and start new colonies the following spring.

GERMAN WASP

VESPULA GERMANICA
Another garden wasp. Look for three black dots on the face to tell it from the Common Wasp.

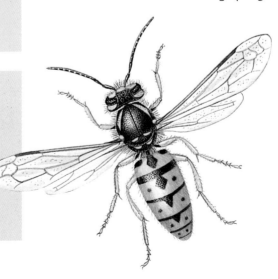

HONEY BEE
APIS MELLIFERA

When to see Spring to autumn.

Where to see Common across Britain and continental Europe. Wild colonies normally nest in holes in trees. Also kept by beekeepers in hives.

What to look for A colony can contain 50,000 bees, including a queen, lots of workers (sterile females) and drones (males). The workers are about 10 mm long; the drones and queens are bigger. The colours vary but the bees are typically brown and hairy, with black and brown striped abdomens. They can sting, but will rarely do so. Honey Bees are very special insects. They are important pollinators, and they make honey.

Honey Bees use a 'waggle dance' to tell other colony members where to find food. The angle of the straight line tells them which direction to go. The length of the line and how much they waggle tells them how far to go.

Did you know?
The combs in a Honey Bee nest are vertical. Those in a wasp's nest are horizontal.

VIOLET CARPENTER BEE
XYLOCOPA VIOLACEA

When to see Spring to autumn, although overwintering adults may be seen earlier in the year on warm days.

Where to see Common in central and southern Europe, but seems to be moving north. A few have been recorded in Britain. The female makes a nest in dead wood, and may make up to three in her lifetime. The adults spend the winter in holes in trees or walls.

What to look for A very big bee, 20–23 mm long. It has a hairy, violet-black body and wonderful violet-blue tinted wings. The males have a yellowish stripe near the tips of their antennae. This bee flies fast and comes to flowers for nectar. It's a gentle giant – it's rare for one to sting.

Did you know?
Violet Carpenter Bees are on the move, very probably because of climate change. They are moving north and there is now a colony in Leicestershire.

TAWNY MINING BEE
ANDRENA FULVA

Did you know?
Tawny Mining Bees live on their own – they are 'solitary' bees. This is very different from wasps, Honey Bees and bumblebees, which live in colonies.

When to see April to July.

Where to see Gardens, parks and open areas in central Europe. Common in southern and eastern England.

What to look for A fairly small bee, measuring about 12 mm in length. The female has a furry orange-brown thorax and abdomen, and a black head. The male is smaller and blackish. Tawny Mining Bees dig underground nests, especially on sandy soils and often in lawns. Look for small piles of soil around an entrance hole. One female may make six nests. She leaves her offspring in a cell filled with food and takes no further interest in it after that. Tawny Mining Bees are important pollinators – look for them feeding on cherry and apple trees, and gooseberry and currant bushes. This is just one of 253 species of mining bee found in Britain and Ireland.

BOMBUS HORTORUM

When to see Late April to October. Most active between June and August.

Where to see Common throughout Britain and other parts of Europe in many habitats, including gardens.

What to look for Fairly large, long-haired bumblebee. Look for a white tail, and yellow at the front and back of the thorax and front of the abdomen. It visits flowers such as cowslips, honeysuckle and foxgloves for nectar. Pollen collects on a bumblebee's 'fur' while it is nectaring – this is 'combed' into pollen baskets on its back legs. About 20–25 mm long.

Garden Bumblebee

Cuckoo Bee

CUCKOO BEE

BOMBUS BARBUTELLUS
Cuckoo bees are related to bumble-bees and survive by gatecrashing a bumblebee nest and laying eggs in it, which the bumblebee then looks after. They normally look like their bumblebee victims, so they're not easy to spot.

Did you know?
The Garden Bumblebee has a very long tongue – about 13.5 mm long. This means that it can get nectar from deeper flowers than other bumblebees.

GREEN TIGER BEETLE
CICINDELA CAMPESTRIS

Did you know?
In an 'insect sprint' this beetle could get the gold – it's one of the fastest running insects there is.

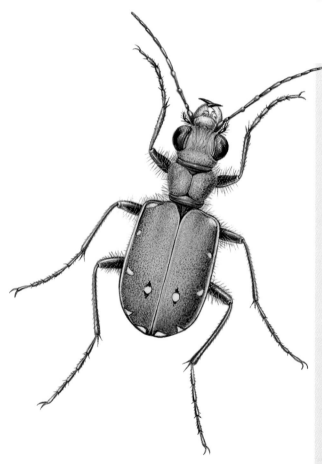

When to see April to September.

Where to see Common in sandy areas, including heaths and sand dunes, throughout Britain and most of continental Europe.

What to look for An eye-catching green beetle with pale spots on its wing cases. Some of the beetles are darker than others, and their markings aren't always the same. They are about 10–15 mm long with long shiny legs, powerful jaws and large eyes. Watch Green Tiger Beetles with care – they might fly off if you get too close! Their long legs also enable them to run away very fast.

VIOLET GROUND BEETLE
CARABUS VIOLACEUS

When to see June to August are especially good for seeing the adult beetles.

Where to see Common in gardens and many other habitats across Britain and much of continental Europe. It's a fierce nocturnal hunter that eats slugs and other minibeasts. To see it during the day, turn over logs and stones carefully – that's where it sleeps.

What to look for A big blue-black beetle, 20–30 mm long. The legs and antennae are long and the wing cases and thorax have shiny purple edges.

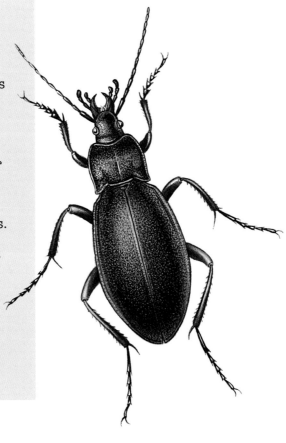

Did you know?

Unlike tiger beetles, Violet Ground Beetles can't fly. Although they are called ground beetles, they will climb up tree trunks when they're hunting.

In daylight many ground beetles take on wonderful metallic green, violet and red colours.

Violet Ground Beetle

Carabus granulatus – another ground beetle

DEVIL'S COACH HORSE
STAPHYLINUS OLENS

Did you know?
This beetle can bite – the bite can hurt and it might even bleed.

When to see Spring to autumn.

Where to see Common across Britain and much of continental Europe in many habitats, including parks, gardens and woods. It's a nocturnal hunter that eats slugs, caterpillars, other minibeasts and carrion. To find it during the daytime check its hideouts – under logs and rubble, for example, or in the compost heap.

What to look for A long, thin black beetle. Its wing cases are small so most of the abdomen is visible, and its hind wings have to be folded up very carefully to fit underneath. If the beetle is threatened, its 'tail' goes up like a scorpion's, its massive jaws open wide and it lets rip with a smelly chemical from its rear! 20–30 mm long. This is one of over 1,000 species of rove beetle in Europe.

When to see April to October. It can be seen during the day and often flies on warm evenings and at night.

Where to see Common across Britain and much of continental Europe in a range of habitats. Will come into gardens. Look for it around cow dung!

What to look for A broad, rounded beetle that is shiny green or blue underneath. Each wing case has seven ridges on it. The legs are thick and hairy. It digs burrows underneath dung and takes it into a chamber at the end of the burrow. The eggs are laid here and the larvae eat the dung. 16–25 mm long.

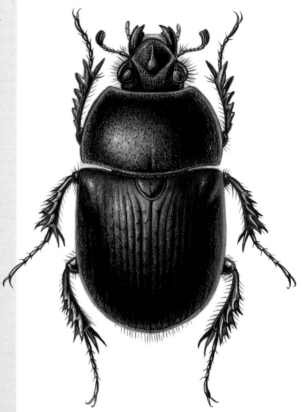

Did you know?

This beetle often has lots of mites on it – that's why it's also known as the Lousy Watchman.

Horned Dung Beetle

Dor Beetle

Dung beetles: trundling waste-disposal units!

COCKCHAFER or MAY BUG
MELOLONTHA MELOLONTHA

When to see May to July or even August. It flies at night.

Where to see Across Britain and other parts of Europe, around gardens, hedgerows and woodlands.

What to look for A chunky, mostly brown beetle with brown legs and wing cases. Lights attract it – the beetle will fly with a thump into lit windows. The thorax and most of the head are black, and there's a pointed black area behind the wing cases too. The male has amazing feathery antennae. 20–30 mm long.

Did you know?
Male Cockchafers use their antennae to 'smell' pheromones, chemicals made by the females.

CLICK BEETLE
ATHOUS HAEMORRHOIDALIS

Did you know?
Click beetle larvae are known as 'wireworms' and can be a serious garden pest.

When to see May to August

Where to see In trees, bushes and grasslands in much of Europe.

What to look for A 'stretched-out', hairy beetle about 10–15 mm long. Look out for its acrobatics. If a beetle finds itself on its back, it bends, and with a click suddenly bends in the other direction, propelling itself up to 30 cm into the air. After a series of mid-air somersaults it lands again – hopefully on its feet. If not, it tries again! One of 69 species of British click beetle.

STAG BEETLE
LUCANUS CERVUS

When to see May to August, particularly on warm evenings.

Where to see Rare in Europe, but still seen in some areas of southern Britain. London is a good place to see Stag Beetles! It's found in woods and parks, but many records are now from gardens. It flies well and is attracted to light.

What to look for A big beetle – at 20–75 mm long, this is the biggest beetle in Europe. Its head and thorax are black, and the wing cases are brown, although they can be nearly black in the female. The 'antlers' are actually jaws – the males fight with them, but don't normally harm each other. Not all males have big antlers – entomologists used to think that small males with small antlers were a different species. Females don't have big antlers, but beware – they are the ones that might bite!

Did you know?

Stag Beetles lay their eggs in rotting wood, especially that of oak trees. It can be five years before the adult emerges, but the adult only lives for a few weeks.

SOLDIER BEETLE
CANTHARIS RUSTICA

Did you know?

They are called soldier beetles because their colours remind people of old-fashioned military uniforms.

When to see May to August.

Where to see Very common throughout Britain. It can be found in damp situations, including woodland edges and open country. Look for it on Umbellifers (plants of the carrot family) such as hogweed.

What to look for A black and orange beetle with a softer exoskeleton and wing cases than most beetles. The wing cases are black, and the legs are black with orange nearest to the body. There is a black spot on the orange area behind the head. The beetle eats other insects, which it finds on flower blooms. Particularly on a sunny day, you might see one flying. About 13 mm long. One of 41 species of soldier beetle in Britain. This one is sometimes called a sailor beetle.

COCINELLA 7-PUNCTATA

When to see March to October

Where to see Found across much of Europe. Very common almost anywhere in Britain.

What to look for This is our most familiar ladybird. Look for red wing cases with seven black spots, one of which is shared between the two wing cases. The front end is black, with two obvious pale patches. The markings don't vary much in this species. The adults and larvae eat aphids, so gardeners like ladybirds. About 5–8 mm long.

Did you know?

Handle ladybirds carefully or they will release a foul-smelling chemical onto you! The chemical comes out of their legs and it is what their warning colours are warning you about.

They hibernate in groups in bark crevices, sheds and houses.

2-SPOT LADYBIRD

ADALIA BIPUNCTATA

A very common red and black ladybird species. It typically has two black spots on red wing cases, but its pattern is much more variable than the 7-spot's. Sometimes, particularly in the north of Britain, the main colour is black rather than red.

22-SPOT LADYBIRD
PSYLLOBORA VIGINTIDUOPUNCTATA

Did you know?

Unlike 7-spot Ladybirds, 22-spots aren't big aphid eaters. Their main food is mildew, a powdery fungus.

When to see April to September, and on warm winter days.

Where to see Occurs throughout Europe. Common in grassy areas in southern Britain, but much harder to find in the north. It spends winter in leaf litter, but may be seen during winter if the weather is mild.

What to look for A yellow and black ladybird. It's yellow with black spots, but despite its name it doesn't always have 22 of them! There are 10 or 11 spots on each wing case. The section in front of the wing cases is called the pronotum. This is yellow too, and has five black spots. It feeds mostly on mildew on Umbellifers (members of the carrot family) and low-growing shrubs. 3–4.5 mm long.

14-SPOT LADYBIRD

PROPYLEA QUATUORDECIMPUNCTATA
Another common yellow and black ladybird, but this one is very variable. It can have anywhere between 4 and 14 spots (although mostly it's 14). The spots can be black on a yellow background or the other way round, and sometimes they join together! Confused?!

HAWTHORN FRUIT or APPLE FRUIT WEEVIL

RHYNCHITES AEQUATUS

Did you know?

This weevil has a two-year life cycle. Its eggs are laid in apples or haws. Then the female chews the stem and the fruit shrivels. The larvae stay in the fruit until autumn, then leave and cover themselves in soil. The adult comes out of the pupa about a year later, but stays underground until spring.

When to see Spring–autumn.

Where to see On hawthorn, apple and other fruit trees in southern Britain and most of continental Europe.

What to look for Small beetle with antennae stuck on its nose! Wing cases can be yellow, red or brown. 2.5–4.5 mm long. There are 416 British species.

WASP BEETLE

CLYTUS ARIETIS

When to see May to August.

Where to see Gardens, woods and hedgerows in most of Europe. Likes hawthorn flowers, Umbellifers, tree trunks, fences and rotting leaves.

What to look for A beetle that pretends to be a wasp for its own protection. It moves like a wasp, too, making the trick even more convincing! But it doesn't have a sting. 5–15 mm long. One of about 70 species of longhorn beetle found in Britain.

Did you know?

The adults may be harmless, but the larvae aren't always. The beetle's eggs are laid in wood (trees or a fence post perhaps), and the tunnels made by the larvae can damage trees.

WHIRLIGIG BEETLE
GYRINUS NATATOR

When to see Almost any time, although it hibernates in pond mud in winter.

Where to see Most of northern and central Europe. Common across Britain. Look for it on ponds, lakes and slow-flowing waterways.

What to look for A small, shiny black beetle whizzing round and round on the water's surface. There are often lots of them together. If disturbed, they dive. The legs are orange and the back two pairs are short and flattened with hairs on the edges to help them swim. About 6 mm long. One of 12 species in Britain.

Did you know?
Whirligig eyes are split into two parts – the top half sees what's happening on the water's surface and the bottom half can watch things under the surface!

VELVET MITE
EUTROMBIDIUM ROSTRATUS

When to see Spring is one of the best times.

Where to see Walls and garden paths.

What to look for A small, red velvety blob. At 3–4 mm long, this is a big mite! Mites are arachnids, like spiders, and like spiders they have eight legs. A spider's body has a waist, though, while a mite's doesn't. This mite has fairly long legs. It's a predator, dining on insects and insect eggs.

Did you know?
You may not have noticed them, but if you have a garden, the chances are that there are millions of mites in it.

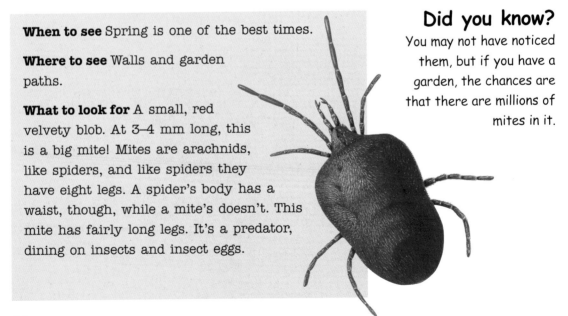

EUROPEAN YELLOW-TAILED SCORPION

EUSCORPIUS FLAVICAUDIS

Did you know?

The first 'British' scorpions were seen in the 1860s and must have arrived in Britain by boat.

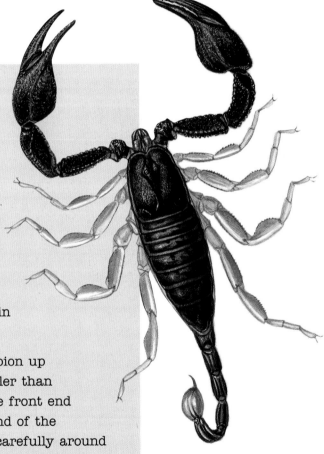

When to see When you're on holiday in southern or central Europe. This scorpion is most active at night, taking cover during the day.

Where to see Mostly found in central and southern Europe, but there are now some in Britain – there's a famous colony at some docks in Kent, and they have also been seen in other places.

What to look for A brown scorpion up to 50 mm long. Its legs are paler than its body, and the pincers at the front end are darker. The sting on the end of the curved tail is yellowish. Look carefully around nooks and crannies in walls – you might see some pincers sticking out. This is a garden species in mainland Europe, and it could become one in Britain too. It's harmless to people, but don't handle it.

HARVESTMAN
PHALANGIUM OPILIO

When to see June to December. It comes out to hunt at night. Survives winter as eggs.

Where to see Across Europe, in low thick vegetation. Also seen on the ground.

What to look for Spider-like with very long legs. Body is one 'blob' with no waist. Female is larger than male – her body could be 10 mm long, his only 3 mm long. Doesn't make silk or venom. One of 23 British species.

Did you know?

Harvestmen will shed a leg (or several!) to escape a predator. That's fine unless they lose their second pair – the tips of which help them to know where they are going.

DADDY-LONG-LEGS SPIDER
PHOLCUS PHALANGIOIDES

When to see All year round.

Where to see Buildings in Europe.

What to look for A pale spider with very long legs. Body has two parts. It hangs upside-down in its web and normally only moves at night, but will wobble up and down very quickly if disturbed. Prey caught in web is wrapped in silk, bitten and injected with poison. Up to about 10 mm long.

Did you know?

Life as a young Daddy-long-legs Spider is risky. If they get too close, a brother or sister might eat them!

GARDEN or CROSS SPIDER
ARANEUS DIADEMATUS

Spiders construct
elaborate webs in
which they catch
their prey.

Did you know?
Eggs are laid in autumn in a clump of
up to 800 by one female. She dies
about a month later and the eggs
hatch in spring.

When to see
June to
November.
It's especially
obvious in
autumn.

Where to see Very
common in Britain and
on the Continent. Found
in gardens, hedges,
woods and heaths. Check
fences, sheds, trees and
bushes for its almost-
circular webs, which can
be 40 cm across. The
spider rests close to its
web during the daylight
hours, and comes out as
it gets
dark.

**What to
look for**
This is a big
spider – the
females are bigger than
the males. A big male
has a body length of
9 mm, but the female's
can be twice this size.
Look for stripy legs and
a white cross pattern on
the abdomen. The base
colour can be anything
from yellowish to pale
brown to orange to dark
brown. The head is pale.

When to see May to September. Sunny days are best.

Where to see Found in most of Europe and common in Britain. Look especially on sun-bathed walls, windowsills, sheds, rocks and smooth tree trunks.

What to look for The Zebra Spider is small but easy to spot. Look for 'zebra stripes' on the abdomen and legs. The two front eyes are very big and beady, making it look quite appealing! The other six eyes are smaller. Unsurprisingly, it has very good eyesight and can detect movement 30 cm away. Zebra Spiders are jumping spiders. They creep up on insects and then jump on them, sometimes from quite a distance away. 5–7 mm long.

Did you know?

Zebra Spiders have eight eyes. Two of them are big and forward facing. This gives them binocular vision and helps them to work out how far to jump to get their next meal!

COMMON WOODLOUSE
ONISCUS ASELLUS

When to see Woodlice are especially common if there is wet weather in spring or autumn. They are most active at night, but can easily be found in their hideaways during the day.

Where to see Common across Britain and other parts of Europe. Woodlice, and this species in particular, like damp places. Rotting trees and compost heaps are worth checking for them, and also look under logs and stones.

What to look for

Woodlice aren't insects – they are Crustaceans and therefore related to crabs and lobsters. This species grows up to 16 mm long. Look for the pale 'edges'. There may be pale spots on its back too. Woodlice have 14 legs. One of about 50 woodlice species found in Britain.

Did you know?

Woodlice have to shed their skins to grow. They do the back half first. Once the new back skin has toughened up they shed the front half.

When moulting, part of woodlouse is pale until new skin toughens up.

PILL WOODLOUSE
ARMADILLIUM VULGARE

Did you know?

This beast is also known as the 'Pill Bug' – and yes, people did once take them as medicine! They were still being swallowed in the 1800s.

When to see This species is active during the day because it is better protected against drying out than some other woodlice.

Where to see Occurs in much of Europe. Common in southern Britain, including in gardens, but harder to find further north. Needs lime for its thick 'shell'. Grasslands on lime (alkaline) soil provide this. Look at the bottoms of walls as well – there's lime in the mortar that's meant to hold the bricks together! Also found under logs, leaves and stones.

What to look for Glossy grey-black body and obviously dome-shaped back. It can roll up into a ball. This protects it from predators and drying out. About 20 mm long.

PILL MILLIPEDE
GLOMERIS MARGINATA

This has more legs, but looks similar to the Pill Woodlouse, especially when it is rolled up. On a rolled up Pill Millipede there's one plate at the back end.

The Pill Woodlouse has a number of smaller plates.

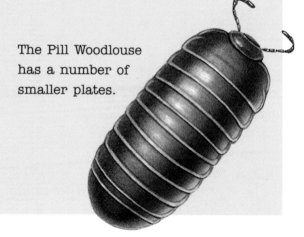

COMMON CENTIPEDE
LITHOBIUS FORFICATUS

Did you know?

Look at this centipede's legs. They get longer and longer as you move from head to tail. That means it can run without tripping over its feet!

When to see A fierce night-time hunter. You can find it during the day by looking under logs, stones and bark.

Where to see Found across Europe, including Britain. Common in many habitats. Look for it in your garden.

What to look for Flattened, glossy golden-brown body with 7 to 15 pairs of legs and only one pair on each segment (millipedes have two pairs per segment). It moves fast (much faster than a millipede), which helps it to catch its animal prey. Its antennae help it to locate prey by smell and touch. 20–30 mm long.

Has long flexible antennae for sensing prey and fangs equipped with venom.

The white Garden Centipede is not actually a centipede, but part of a group called the Symphylans.

Geophilus carpophagus – a very flexible common centipede.

COMMON FLAT-BACKED MILLIPEDE

POLYDESMUS ANGUSTUS

When to see Most active at night. Also on spring and early summer afternoons.

Where to see Found over most of Europe. Common in Britain. Look for it in compost heaps and under rotting leaves.

What to look for It looks flattened, but its body is actually more or less circular (typical of millipedes), with flat plates on the back. It is brown and blotchy with pale legs. Although it has up to 74 legs, it's a slow mover. The adults have 20 segments and nearly all of the segments have two pairs of legs. Unlike centipedes, millipedes are mostly vegetarian. 20–25 mm long. One of about 50 British millipede species.

Did you know?

Even millipedes that live in dark places are most active at night. They are probably woken up by small drops in temperature.

Some millipedes have clusters of very small eyes and short antennae that touch and stroke the ground in front of them as they amble along.

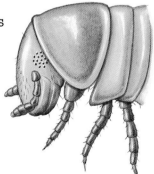

SOME BUG WORDS

Abdomen The rear part of an insect's or arachnid's body.

Arachnid An animal in the class Arachnida, which includes spiders, harvestmen, scorpions and mites.

Binocular vision Viewing things with two eyes, so that they are seen in 3-D and distances can be estimated.

Carrion Dead animals.

Chrysalis What a caterpillar becomes before turning into an adult butterfly or moth. Also known as a pupa.

Crustacean An animal in the class 'Crustacea', which includes crabs, lobsters and woodlice.

Drone The male of an insect that lives in a colony, such as a Honey Bee.

Exoskeleton A skeleton on the outside of the body.

Habitat The place in which a plant or animal lives, e.g. woodland or a pond.

Larva (plural: larvae) What comes out of most insect eggs. Most insects are larvae before they become adults.

Mimicry Copying or pretending to be something else.

Moult An animal coming out of an exoskeleton so that it can grow.

Nymph Similar to larva but refers to insects that don't have a pupa or chrysalis in their lifecycle.

Ovipositor A tool for laying eggs.

Pheromone A chemical that may be used to attract a mate.

Pollen A powder made by the male part of a flower or a male cone.

Pollen basket A 'basket' on the back legs of bumblebees and Honey Bees used to collect pollen.

Pollinator An animal that carries pollen from the male part of a flower to the female part. Most are insects.

Pupa (plural: pupae) What happens after larva and before adult in insects where larva looks very different from adult. See also chrysalis.

Queen One form of the female in insects that live in colonies, such as ants and Honey Bees. Queens are able to lay eggs. See also Worker.

Thorax Middle part of an insect's body.

Wing cases The hard front wings of beetles that cover the soft back wings when the wings are folded.

Worker In insects such as ants and Honey Bees, workers are females that can't lay eggs and do lots of work! In some insect species there are male workers too.

SPOTTED!

You can use the boxes opposite the bug names on this page to tick off the species you have spotted.

Silverfish	❏	Garden Bumblebee	❏
Two-tailed Bristletail	❏	Cuckoo Bee	❏
Pond Olive	❏	Green Tiger Beetle	❏
Common Blue Damselfly	❏	Violet Ground Beetle	❏
Large Red Damselfly	❏	Devil's Coach Horse	❏
Southern Hawker	❏	Dor Beetle	❏
Common Field Grasshopper	❏	Cockchafer	❏
Blue-winged Grasshopper	❏	Click Beetle	❏
Speckled Bush Cricket	❏	Stag Beetle	❏
Praying Mantis	❏	Soldier Beetle	❏
Common Earwig	❏	7-spot Ladybird	❏
Common Green Shield Bug	❏	2-spot Ladybird	❏
Common Green Capsid	❏	22-spot Ladybird	❏
Common Pond Skater	❏	14-spot Ladybird	❏
Water Scorpion	❏	Hawthorn Fruit Weevil	❏
Great Water Boatman	❏	Wasp Beetle	❏
Common Froghopper	❏	Whirligig Beetle	❏
Green Lacewing	❏	Velvet Mite	❏
Caddis Fly	❏	European Yellow-tailed Scorpion	❏
Common Crane Fly	❏	Harvestman	❏
St Mark's Fly	❏	Daddy-long-legs Spider	❏
Bee Fly	❏	Garden Spider	❏
Celery Fly	❏	Zebra Spider	❏
Hoverfly	❏	Common Woodlouse	❏
Bluebottle	❏	Pill Woodlouse	❏
Horntail	❏	Pill Millipede	❏
Bedeguar Gall Wasp	❏	Common Centipede	❏
Ichneumon Fly	❏	Common Flat-backed Millipede	❏
Small Black Ant	❏		
Red Ant	❏		
Common Wasp	❏		
German Wasp	❏		
Honey Bee	❏		
Violet Carpenter Bee	❏		
Tawny Mining Bee	❏